The Pub

Norman Cristofoli

Norman Cristofoli

Copyright © Norman Cristofoli, 2020

norman.cristofoli@gmail.com

normancristofoli.com

Cover art by Richard Mongiat

richardmongiat.com

ISBN (print) 978-0-9813875-7-4
ISBN (EPUB) 978-0-9813875-8-1
ISBN (MOBI) 978-0-9813875-9-8

This book was produced through CanamBooks.

This book is available for purchase on the CanamBooks Store:
www.canambooks.com/store

The Set

The scene is an old, run down pub. Depending on the country and culture where the play is produced, this venue/scene can be a tavern, bar or other establishment. Everything in the Pub should be well worn, used and verging on dilapitated.

The bar is in the rear centre of the stage in the shape of a squared "U" with a space for the entrance on the rear left. Glasses hang from various areas around the bar, old pictures on faded patterned wallpaper adorn the walls. A number of small tables and chairs are spread around the stage.

There are three doors; one at stage front right and one directly opposite at stage front left. The third door is at the back left of the stage with a sign above it that says "Toilets" (or comparable term).

Characters may be of any nationality, however, their genders must be as set out in the play, with the exception of Sally Crow, who can be female, transgender female or transvestite.

Cast of Characters

Paul Satin

Victoria King

Jon James and the Monk – are played by same actor.

Sally Crow

Hiram Digger and Fred Munzigar – are played by
same actor

Harry Hood

Sam Johansen, Jake Javelin and Elvis Presley impersonator
– played by same actor

Eric Johnson

Boris Neil

The Doorman

Cloaked Figure

Character Profiles

Paul Satin is based on the historical figure of Saint Paul the Apostle, just prior to his conversion on the road to Damascus. The character represents the personage of Saul of Tarsus (original name) who was an active participant in the persecution of early Christians. Saul was a Jew, but also a Roman citizen and was taught to worship the Roman deities. At this point in his life, he was a human that was deeply conflicted in his beliefs and skeptical of all answers put forth to him.

Victoria King was inspired by Queen Victoria of England during the period of her life immediately after the death of her husband Prince Albert. Their love was so widely noted that when Albert died after 20 years of marriage, Victoria became despondent and tried to seclude herself from the world. She was someone who had found love, and when he was gone, all she had left was her duty as the Queen.

Jon James is based on the American cult leader Jim Jones who founded the "People's Temple." Jones was infamous for the 918 murder-suicides of the cult's members in Jonestown, Guyana by cyanide poisoning mixed with "Kool-Aid." Jones died from a gunshot wound to the head; it is suspected his death was a suicide.

Sally Crow was inspired by the English occultist, ceremonial magician and writer Aleister Crowley. He founded the religion and philosophy of Thelema, identifying himself as the prophet entrusted with guiding humanity into the early 20th century. A man of sharp wit and a wry sense of humour, he was labeled the "Wickedest Man in the World" for his dalliances with the occult.

Hiram Digger is based on German philosopher Martin Hiedigger who is best known for his contributions to Phenomenology and the beginnings of Existentialism.

Fred Munzigar was inspired by the Austrian psychologist and neurologist Sigmund Freud, known for his work in the development of psychoanalysis.

Harry Hood was inspired by the American illusionist and escape artist Harry Houdini. In the later years of his life, Houdini was noted for the debunking of fake spiritualists. However, Houdini's crusade against charlatans was based on his own search for spiritual answers, which included the quest to reach beyond the veil of death and contact the spiritual world.

Sam Johansen is based on Samuel Johnson, the English writer, essayist, moralist, literary critic, and composer of *"A Dictionary of the English Language."*

Jake Javelin is based on William Shakespeare, the English playwright and poet, widely regarded as the greatest writer in the English language and the world's pre-eminent dramatist. All of Jakes lines are direct quotes from Shakespearean plays which are noted in the parentheses (which may or may not be part of the performance).

Eric Johnson was inspired by John Merrick, the Englishman born with severe deformities and who was exhibited as a human curiosity nick-named the "Elephant Man." He was a meek but intelligent individual who dealt with a life of disability and disfigurement.

Boris Neil was inspired by the Danish physicist Niels Bohr who made foundational contributions to understanding atomic structure and quantum theory. Niels Bohr was also a philosopher and promoter of scientific research.

The Monk was inspired by a long list of religious and fanatical cult followers throughout history. Through his appearance, he is also meant to introduce the concepts of reincarnation and past lives into the general theories of discussion. It is important that the two characters (portrayed by the same actor) are identifiable as the same.

The Doorman: The concept for the Doorman is for him to be dressed in uniform. The author would see him as a traditional "London Bobby" from the 1920's era, but any other authoritarian uniform would suffice.

Cloaked Figure – Director's choice – the character of the cloaked figure can be any of the previous actors who are now offstage, or can be someone the Director has brought in for this small part. The Cloaked Figure can be male, female, young or old and of any ethnic persuasion.

The Pub

Act One

(The lights on stage are dimly lit while the curtain remains closed. The curtain opens to reveal the actors on stage frozen in their positions. Sally the barmaid cleaning a glass, Sam sitting rear stage left doing a crossword puzzle, Hiram Digger by the bar talking to Sally. Victoria King, Jon James and Paul Satin sitting centre stage. Stage lights flash on and everyone comes to life.)

Paul: *(looking around confused)* Where am I?

Jon: In the Pub.

Paul: *(looks at Jon)* How did I get here?

Jon: You weren't here, then you were.

Paul: Why am I here?

Jon: *(sarcastically)* Yeah sure, why don't we start with the easy questions.

Paul: *(looking around)* What . . . what . . . I don't get it, what am I doing here?

Jon: Well, there have been many theories, but I guess the most obvious answer is that you are just simply passing time while you wait for your name to be called.

Paul: Sorry, can we start over, I'm confused.

Jon: Try not to worry about it, name your poison.

Paul: Huh?

Jon: What are you drinking? You know, alcohol, the stuff that helps you forget what you can't remember to begin with.

Paul: Oh, ah . . .

Victoria: Whatever you do don't order the Kool-aid.

Paul: Uh, okay, I'll have a beer.

Jon: Comin' right up. *(he gets up, goes to the bar and orders)*

Hiram: *(turning to Jon)* You know Jon, I generally disagree with almost everything you say but I have to admit that the best thing about Irish whiskey is that it helps you forget what memory hasn't already lost, yet it often also helps one to remember the true self that we often hide.

Sally: I don't think that makes any sense.

Hiram: You're right, it is insensible, like life. So please pour me another glass of illogical delusion.

Jon: I'll have two pints please.

Paul: *(to Victoria)* Excuse me, but I still don't understand how I got here or even where "here" is.

Victoria: It's like that sometimes. It's just a matter of getting used to it.

Paul: Getting used to what?

Victoria: Waiting.

Paul: Waiting for what?

Victoria: Waiting for your name to be called.

Paul: Why?

Victoria: That's when you leave.

Paul: For where?

Victoria: I don't know.

Paul: Then why go?

Victoria: There isn't any choice.

Paul: Why not?

Victoria: *(getting a little irritated)* I don't know. You ask too many questions.

Paul: And you don't seem to have any answers.

Victoria: Do you?

Paul: *(apologetically)* No, you're right, I'm sorry for pressing.

Victoria: Accepted.

Paul: My name is Paul . . . Paul Satin.

Victoria: We are Victoria.

Paul: We?

Victoria: Yes, We.

(Pause, in which two people sit in an uncomfortable silence.)

Jon: *(to Sally and Hiram)* I'm telling you that this is but one part of the journey. There is so much more.

Hiram: Why do we have to believe that there must be more? And with that belief, we accept our present lot with the hope that there will be another time, another pub, another situation, another chance.

Sally: *(speaks while pouring drinks)* What if this is our second chance.

What if this is our only chance.

Should we not follow our dreams and cherish this life.

Should we not evaluate ourselves, spiritually, intellectually and physically.

Should we not treat each and every moment with intense honesty.

Jon: This existence is no accident. There is an intelligent design and each of us is a small part of it.

Hiram: You cannot depend on some deity to answer your questions and judge your fate. Inventing a deity only allows you the opportunity to blame that deity for your misfortunes.

Jon: Things happen for a reason.

Sally: Why?

Jon: It's all part of the Supreme Being's plan.

Hiram: *(to Jon)* So many people have come through this Pub and you believe that the Proprietor has a plan for each and every one of them. Let me see, does it go something like this: "Spend your life in selfish consumption of the earth's natural resources . . . and then die." Some plan.

Jon: I believe that there is something far greater than our experience in this Pub. Belief gives people hope when they have to cope with the problems they are facing. People need to believe that the pain and suffering that they are going through will give birth to happier times, meaningful experiences, spiritual insights, new found wisdom, maybe even love.

Sally: We grow, we change, we never stay the same.
            Things don't happen for a reason, unless the
            Supreme Beings are putting together puzzles.

Victoria: *(to Paul)* Sometimes We contemplate the same
            questions and We must admit that the lack of
            meaningful answers is somewhat frustrating.

Paul: Are there answers?

Victoria: We believe there are. If there wasn't, then what
            would be the point.

Sam: Does anyone know a four letter word that
            means predestined come-uppance?

Hiram: Fate!

Sam: Thank you. I kinda guessed that would be the
            answer but was looking for validation before I
            committed it to paper.

Jon: *(returning with drinks)* Here's your poison,
            cheers.

Paul: Thanks.

Jon: So what do you think of this place.

Paul: I'm not sure.

Jon: It's not too bad, it's got ambience. It's got that
            old, worn-in, comfortable feeling, like a well
            used couch. I've always wanted a place like this
            of my own. It gives me a peaceful warm feeling.

Victoria: It gives us unmentionable digestion. Excuse us.
            (she gets up and goes to the toilet)

Paul: What's with her and the "we" and "us" stuff?

Jon: I think it has something to do with divine
            privilege bestowed upon special people.

Paul: Is she special?

Jon: Oh yes . . . she's very special.

Paul: Listen, ah what's your name?

Jon: James, Jon James, and you are?

Paul: Paul Satin. Listen Jon, I'm confused. What's
          really going on here?

Jon: How do you mean?

Paul: Well, like this Pub, who built it?

Jon: The owner I guess, the proprietor, the landlord.
          It's hard to pin them down with a name. Again,
          there are so many theories.

Paul: And who is the Proprietor?

Jon: I don't know.

Paul: Does anybody?

Jon: No one that I have ever met has been able to
          offer definitive proof.

Paul: *(a little irritated)* This is absurd. What the hell is
          going on here!

Jon: Everything goes on here.

Paul: Like what?

Jon: Well there's food and drink, conversation,
          existence.

Paul: And then what?

Jon: Well, eventually the Doorman calls your name
          and you leave.

Paul: The Doorman?

Jon: Yes, the Doorman. He comes in that door over there *(pointing stage left)* and calls your name.

Paul: *(leaning over table)* Where does the Doorman take us?

Jon: Out the door.

Paul: That's it! Just out the door!

Jon: Listen Paul, nobody truly knows the answers. We've all asked the same questions but the only answers up to now have been unbridled speculation.

Paul: Okay, okay, this conversation is ridiculous, I need something more substantial.

Jon: Alright then, let me ask you a question. Do you know what Genghis Khan's name was?

Paul: Huh, I don't understand.

Jon: Do you know what Genghis Khan's name was?

Paul: Genghis Khan I suppose.

Jon: Wrong! His name was Temujin. Khan means Chief and Genghis Khan means Universal Chief or ruler. It's a simple mistake that many people make with names and titles of people.

Paul: What has this got to do with why we are here?

Jon: It just goes to show you that things aren't always they way they seem. You think you know something and then it turns out to be something else.

Paul: So?

Jon: *(looking around not wanting to be heard)* I think this place is a test.

Paul: A test for what?

Jon: A test by the Supreme Being.

Paul: You're kidding me, right?

Jon: It's the most logical explanation. The Supreme Being needs to know if we are worthy.

Paul: (pausing, looking cynical) Are you suffering from a severe allergy to logic and common sense.

Jon: Don't you believe in the Supreme Being?

Paul: I don't know what to believe.

Jon: Why?

Paul: Why? Look around you. Here we are in this old, worn down pub. We don't know why we're here, where we came from or what's going to happen to us. According to you, our only surety is that some Doorman is eventually going to call our names and that we are to accompany him to who knows where. Now you want me to believe that some benevolent or malevolent deity has created this just to test us. It doesn't make sense, there isn't a single sign, a notice, a doormat, a bar towel or anything that would even make me contemplate a Supreme Owner … Proprietor … Being Thing.

Jon: That's just the point. If the Supreme Being wanted to test us, wouldn't it be logical to create the ideal situation not to believe in him.

Paul: Or maybe you're just nuts.

Jon: Be careful, the Supreme Being could be watching us now.

Sam: What is a six letter word that is an alternate name for man's paradise?

Sally: Vagina.

Hiram: Sally, you naughty girl. The word he's looking for is Utopia.

Sally: Same thing.

Sam: Thank you. They both fit.

(Victoria re-enters and goes to the bar to order a drink.)

Victoria: White wine please.

Sally: Coming right up your highness. So tell me what it is that you do?

Victoria: We are into real estate.

Sally: *(sarcastically)* Oh, I'm sorry, couldn't they find a cure.

Hiram: *(laughing)* Ooooh, Sally, you are so wicked.

(Victoria accepts her drink, gives Sally a cool stare and then rejoins Paul and Jon.)

Victoria: *(with mild sarcasm)* Has he been exploring his ideas with you.

Paul: Yes, unfortunately.

Jon: Paul, don't cut me short, I know what I'm talking about.

Victoria: *(to Paul)* That's what he keeps telling us over and over.

Sally: *(laughing)* Hiram, your sense of humour is simply perverse. I love it.

Hiram: If you think that's bad, wait till you hear the one about the horny shepherd that's allergic to wool. *(laughing)*

Victoria: Hiram, please come and join us, make us laugh.

(Hiram walks over to their table.)

Jon: *(to Paul)* This is Hiram. He's a man of questionable humor. Hiram, this is Paul.

Hiram: Pleased to meet you. *(holds out his hand to shake and when Paul goes to return the shake Hiram quickly pulls his hand away)* Ha! Works every time.

Paul: Is everybody around here nuts?

Hiram: Come now, don't get discouraged. Live one moment at a time is what I say. And since the moment I've arrived, not once have I ever failed to satisfy an audience.

Paul: Where do you usually perform?

Hiram: Wherever I am.

Paul: What about the audience?

Hiram: *(turning to look at the audience)* Whoever is watching . . . even if it is but for a fleeting moment.

Victoria: Hiram, We could have used you earlier when We needed a humorous story.

Hiram: Victoria my dear, you know my heart soars whenever you feel charitable enough to toss me but a moment of your attention.

Victoria: Thank you Hiram, We are grateful.

Jon: What a load of crap.

Hiram: *(to Jon)* You wouldn't know the difference between beauty and crap if you had to do a taste test. Here in front of you is beauty and grace, one of the finest creatures my eyes have ever beheld, but you just sit there and ponder worthless questions about your destiny. Why care so much about your philosophical tests when you have Helen of Troy, Venus deMilo and Cleopatra here before you to desire.

Jon: You're a ludicrous old man. You talk as if you expect to live your life minute by minute with no plans for the future.

Hiram: I live my life second by passing second. How can YOU plan for the future when you don't even live in the moment.

Jon: The future is where everything lies.

Hiram: The future only holds what you can accomplish in the present.

Jon: You're just a bitter old man.

Hiram: Of course I'm bitter, I've had to deal with assholes my whole life.

Jon: Are you calling me an asshole?

Hiram: Marvelous! You finally got something right. I was afraid that you wouldn't understand this little reparté that we've been having.

Victoria: Will both of you please stop.

Paul: I find this rather amusing.

Victoria: We are tired of hearing it. We are tired of thinking about it.

Jon: But Victoria, this is important.

Hiram: Victoria, my humblest apologies. What can I do
            to redeem myself before your eyes. Let me be
            the court jester for your pleasure. *(Suddenly
            lighting up with a new idea)* Shall I sing for you?

Jon: Oh dear, not again.

Victoria: Yes Hiram, please sing and dance for us.

Paul: I hope it's more entertaining than that
            handshake.

Hiram: Sir, I'm a passable dancer and a moderate
            voice.

Paul: Do you need accompaniment or do you always
            play your own tune?

Hiram: I need no one and everyone.

Jon: You want that as your epitaph.

Victoria: Hiram, don't listen to them, please . . . please
            dance for us.

Hiram: Alright then, let me see if I remember.
            (sings and does a soft shoe dance)

            How does one measure
            the quality of life
            Is it measured by joy
            or is it measured by strife

            Is it measured in comparison
            with the life of others
            the conquests we have made
            or by a collection of lovers

Do we compare with the famous
And if so, who?
Gandhi? Napoleon?
The one beside you?

Or is it simply measured
by the deeds that you have done
the things you have created
the tournaments you have won

But alas my friends
This I must relate
Only you can determine
what is to be your fate

You can only be as happy
as the wisdom you fulfill
the achievements you have set
and formed by your will

Quality of life should be
as you would dream of living
with grateful acceptance
and charitable forgiving

(continues dancing)

Jon: *(mockingly)* Ludicrous and blasphemous.

Hiram: *(still dancing)* Thank you, thank you, I take
           pleasure in seeing you squirm before the truth.

(Stage door left bursts open and the Doorman walks in.)

Doorman: Digger, Hiram Digger

Hiram: Oh damn, may I at least finish my dance.

Doorman: Mister Digger you must come now.

Hiram: Alright. Victoria my dear, maybe I'll dance for you again when you join me in the next room.

Paul: *(standing up quickly)* What do you mean in the next room! Do you know where you are going, where the Doorman takes you?

Hiram: Of course.

Paul: Why didn't you tell us?

Hiram: You didn't ask.

Doorman: *(sternly)* Mr. Digger, please come now.

Hiram: Coming, coming.

(They head out the door.)

Paul: *(chasing after them)* Wait!

(The door slams in Paul's face. Paul tries the handle but the door is locked. He tries pulling on the door but he can't open it. He stops and contemplates a moment, turns and walks across the stage, and tries the door on stage right. It too is locked.)

Jon: You'll never get them open, we've tried.

(Paul stops, looks around the bar thinking.)

Paul: How did you come to be here.

Jon: I walked in through that door *(pointing to stage right)*.

Paul: But where were you before you came in that door?

Jon: On the other side of it.

Paul: Stop being facetious, just answer the question.

Jon: I did.

Paul: Your answers are a load of crap!

Sam: Nope. Crap is just four letters. I need an eight letter word that means misrepresentation by deceit.

Sally: Religion.

Victoria: Politics.

Jon: Paganism.

Paul: Bull Shit.

Sam: Is Bullshit one word?

Paul: If it fits, who cares.

Sam: Good point.

Victoria: Paul, does it really matter so much where you came from or where you end up when your name is called.

Paul: Yes, it matters to me.

Victoria: Why?

Paul: *(after thinking a moment)* I just can't accept that this is all there is without some sort of logical reason or definable meaning.

Victoria: And what if there is no answer.

Paul: If there is no reason or meaning, then so be it. It may not be the perfect answer but at least it's an answer.

Jon: Listen Paul, I knew this Rock and Roll star once. A real friendly guy he was. He used to give everyone free copies of his records. One day The Doorman called his name, he said goodbye and was gone.

The next day the barmaid found all those free records in the garbage. People had only kept them to be polite and friendly because he was such a nice guy.

Paul: What's the point?

Jon: Not everyone is interested in your quest for the meaning of life, and conversely, not everyone is suitable for my answers.

Paul: You know, you should take an antihistamine for that allergy.

Victoria: Paul, We can sympathize, but whatever it is you're looking for may or may not be here.

Paul: It's got to be. Hiram seemed to know.

Victoria: What if there isn't any way to find out the ultimate answers? Shouldn't we resolve to make the best of our situations.

Paul: Has anybody asked the Doorman?

Jon: The Doorman only speaks to the person he's calling.

Paul: *(pointing to Sally)* What about her?

(They all turn and look to Sally who has her back to the audience, cleaning glasses.)

Paul: *(walking up to the bar)* Excuse me.

Sally: Yes, what would you like?

Paul: I'd like to know where the Doorman takes us.

Sally: I'm sorry, but I don't know.

Paul: How long have you been working here?

Sally: Oh, a long time now. I suppose since I got here.

Paul: Well, who's your boss, who owns the place?

Sally: The Proprietor.

Paul: And who is the Proprietor?

Sally: The one who built the joint I guess.

Paul: How did you get the job?

Sally: Well, I came in through that door like everybody else. While I was waiting, the Barmaid before me was called by the Doorman. Another chap approached me and said he was one of the Proprietor's assistants and asked if I wanted the job.

Paul: So you actually never met this Proprietor.

Sally: Well . . . .

Paul: Is there something else?

Sally: There was this one time I thought it might have been him but I don't know for sure.

Paul: Please, tell me about it, what happened?

Sally: Once this gentleman came in and sat over in that corner *(pointing stage right)*. When I asked him what he wanted, he looked up at me and said "Buddhists do not have visions of the Christ; and Christians do not have visions of Mohamed; and Muslims don't see apparitions of the Buddha. Could it be that they each have a vision of the Divine, and merely clothe them in the vestiges of their fashion." Then the Doorman came in and beckoned him with a silent motion of his hand and he left.

Paul: That's it? You didn't ask him what all of this is supposed to mean.

Sally: It never crossed my mind.

Paul: Well that was rather moronic.

Sally: *(after a pause)* We all have deficiencies and we all have strengths. If all you see are the deficiencies . . . . then maybe you need to take a giant leap up the evolutionary scale.

Paul: *(stopping for a moment)* You're quite right, my apologies, I'll have a gin and tonic, thanks.

Sally: You're welcome.

Paul: If he ever comes in again will you point him out to me.

Sally: *(as she hands him the drink)* Sure, I'll be glad to. *(as he reaches into his pocket to pay)* Oh, don't worry about paying, I'll just put it on your tab.

(Paul leaves Sally and walks toward Jon & Victoria.)

Jon: *(in mocking anticipation)* Well, what did she say?

Paul: Nothing, just more theories. *(looking around)* How about him? *(nodding towards Sam)*

Victoria: We doubt if you'll learn anything more from him.

Jon: Paul, why don't you stop chasing your tail and look at my answers for awhile. You might find them very revealing after you've thought about them.

Paul: No, thank you, I don't think I'd like them at all.

Jon: Then you are a fool, because I know the way.

Victoria: Jon, you're a nice enough guy, but you've really got a complex about yourself.

Jon: The offer still stands you know. It will always be open to you.

Victoria: No thank you.

Paul: What offer?

Vicotria: He wants us to come and be the Pearly Queen at his own Pub.

Paul: *(pausing and then looking over at Jon)* You are nuts.

Jon: I'm offering a viable alternative.

Paul: Yeah right, now what about that guy *(pointing to Sam).*

Victoria: He's no different from the rest of us.

Paul: Well, I think I'll ask him anyway.

(Paul walks over to Sam.)

Paul: Hi, my name's Paul.

Sam: Hello, I am Sam Johansen.

Paul: What are you doing?

Sam: A crossword puzzle.

Paul: Looks like fun.

Sam: It's words. We need words.

Paul: Mind if I ask you a couple of questions.

Sam: I will respond to your words with words of my own.

Paul: Do you know where we are?

Sam: *(stating the obvious)* In a Pub.

Paul: Do you know . . . .

(Stage door left opens and Doorman walks in.)

Doorman: Johansen, Samuel Johansen.

(Sam gets up and starts to go to the door. Paul rushes to the door and stands between Sam and the Doorman.)

Paul: *(to Doorman)* Excuse me, I'm wondering if you could answer a couple of questions for me.

Doorman: Mr. Johansen, it's time to go.

Paul: Please, hold on a minute, I just want to ask one question.

Doorman: Mr. Johansen.

Sam: Excuse me, I've got to go.

Paul: I just want to know where you take us, that's all.

Doorman: *(sternly)* Mr. Johansen!

Sam: Hey, don't get him mad, he's taking me, not you.

(Paul grabs Sam's arm as he tries to walk by.)

Paul: No! Wait!

(Sam pulls his arm free and walks with the Doorman out the door.)

Jon: Nice try, now what are you gonna do for an encore?

Paul: *(angrily walking towards Jon)* I might just come over there and bloody your nose.

(Stage door right opens and in walks Harry Hood. Harry goes to the bar and orders a drink. Paul, Victoria and Jon watch him.)

Harry: I'll have a vodka, with just a little ice.

Sally: Comin' up.

Harry: You know, I knew this musician once. A real friendly guy he was. Used to give away copies of his records. Well one day he was gone and by the following evening the garbage was filled with his life's work.

Sally: Some people just don't like music.

Harry: Yeah, I guess you're right. *(Harry notices the stares of the others and goes over to join them)* Hello, my name is Harry.

Victoria: We are Victoria.

Jon: *(to Harry)* Do you believe in the Supreme Being?

Harry: I haven't decided yet.

Jon: Don't waste any time, it's a very important question. I'd like to talk to you about it when you've got a free moment.

Paul: You're really beginning to bug me Jon.

Jon: And you're a blind man looking in the mirror.

Paul: What about you Vic, I'd really like to know what you think.

Victoria: Our name is Victoria and We would rather not say anything.

Paul: Why?

Victoria: Our beliefs are private and that is how We wish
             them to remain.

Harry: Sounds good to me.

Paul: You stay out of it.

Harry: That's fine with me too. Excuse me Victoria,
             would you like to see some card tricks? *(pulls a
             deck of cards from his pocket)*

Victoria: Anything would be more enjoyable than
             listening to these two argue about what they
             can't answer to begin with. *(she gets up and
             moves to another table with Harry)*

Sally: Can I watch too, I love card tricks. Are they
             Tarot cards?

Harry: *Sure, why not. (Sally comes round to sit with
             Victoria and Harry)*

Jon: Listen Paul, we have to make a stand for what
             we know is right.

Paul: I don't know what's right, so why do I have to
             make a stand for anything.

Jon: At least with Hiram, he stood for something,
             even though the something he stood for was
             senseless to me. But you . . . you run around
             saying "Why are we here?" and when someone
             gives you an answer, you turn around and slap
             them in the face. What kind of reasoning is
             that? At least I offer an alternative.

Paul: Sorry Jon, but what you seem to offer sounds
             like nonsense to me.

Jon: What I offer is peace and happiness.

Paul: What!?

Jon: I've thought it all out. I'm going to open my own pub.

Paul: *(laughing)* Now I know you're nuts.

Jon: *(loudly)* Why? Why is it so crazy to want to reach for the ultimate. I'm quite capable of running my own establishment.

Victoria: Oh hell, here we go again.

Jon: That's right, here we go again and I think you should damn well listen. I'm going to start my own Pub and it's going to be run my way. No Doorman, no mysterious Proprietor. There'll be plenty for everyone, modern conveniences, comfortable furniture. It'll be a paradise.

Harry: What'll it cost to get in?

Jon: All you have to do is love.

Harry: Love who?

Jon: Love me.

Harry: That's a rather steep price.

Jon: It'll be a private Pub, by invitation only. You might not even get invited.

Harry: Who is?

Jon: Whomever I want to invite. It'll be my Pub and there'll only be one rule, love me, that's all. I'll offer paradise in return for your love and obedience.

Harry: That's two rules.

Jon: Rules, rules, who gives a damn about rules.

Harry: Rules come in handy, especially for the
            Rulemaker.

Jon: You want rules, fine! I'll give you one *(pointing
            to Harry)* you're not invited.

Harry: *(mockingly)* Darn, and I've already rented a tux
            for the opening.

(The others laugh.)

Jon: Laugh, go ahead and laugh, you'll all be sorry.
            You're going to end up in a tortuous evil
            cesspit. That's where the Doorman takes you. I
            know, I've had a vision. I can save you but you
            don't want to be saved. Only those that follow
            me will be saved. Only those that love me will
            be freed from the bonds of eternal misery.
            Only those . . . .

Paul: Dammit Jon, shut up!!!

*(Jon stops, regains his composure and walks to the bar.
Sally goes to serve him.)*

Sally: *(to Jon)* What can I get you?

Jon: I need some sanity for this asylum.

Sally: Sorry, I don't have that on tap or in a bottle.

Paul: *(to Victoria and Harry)* There ought to be a law
            against people like that.

Victoria: Please Paul, you mustn't be so hard.

Paul: But the guy's a total headcase.

Harry: The man is highly ego-centric, but it doesn't
            mean he has to be silenced.

Paul: A minute ago you were the one leading the
            charge, now you're defending him.

Harry: I'm not defending him. I'm defending his right to have his own opinions.

Paul: *(submitting with a huff)* Alright, that I can accept. It's just that sometimes I get so angry. Everything inside of me just boils up and I get so, so. . . .

Harry: Frustrated.

Victoria: Don't think about it so much. The more you bang your head against the wall, the more it will hurt, until you become so numb that you won't know anything.

Paul: *(to Harry)* What's your answer.

Harry: I don't have answers.

Paul: You just do card tricks.

Harry: Tricks are for relaxation and picking up girls.

Victoria: Oh really.

Harry: Curses, honesty foils me again.

Paul: Cut the wit Harry. You're holding something back.

Harry: Always.

Paul: I barely know you, yet I sense something, like an air of mystery.

Harry: I'll take that as a compliment.

Paul: What is it Harry, what's so special?

Harry: Well, if you really want to know, I'm a Spiritual Escapist.

Paul: I think I'm about to be sorry I asked.

Victoria: Paul, don't always be so skeptical. We agree
            that Jon is probably delusional but you seem
            to want everything to be black and white.

Paul: (*smiling*) And you're a happy medium.

Harry: No, that's my line of work.

Paul: What?

Harry: A Medium.

Paul: What, you want to make contact with ghosts?

Harry: If I can.

Paul: Maybe you should be talking to Jon.

Harry: Paul, I would also like to know why we are here.
            However, you seem to want to close all avenues
            without ever walking down the street.

Paul: Like Jon's dead end.

Harry: Not all roads are one-way. I once travelled
            through that realm of consciousness and I
            found that I wasn't satisfied with what I found.
            But at least I explored and searched before I
            made any decisions. To some people, like Jon,
            it's exactly what they want.

Victoria: We are generally not the exploring kind, but
            We don't eliminate someone that is. Paul, you
            want to find answers and We respect you for
            that, We'll even help you if We can, but you
            can't go looking for answers only in the places
            you want to look. You have to explore the slums
            as well as the palaces.

Paul: I'm sorry Victoria, but I'm a realist. The only place I can look for answers is in reality, here in this pub and the only two other places that I know of are on the other side of either of those doors.

Victoria: But how will you find answers in this reality, and you can't go through the doors until it's your time.

Paul: So where does that leave me, except for banging my head against the wall.

Harry: There are other places to search.

Paul: Where?

Harry: Inside of yourself.

Paul: What, you mean like internal organs . . . liver, spleen, gall bladder?

Harry: *(pauses and speaks with serious tone)* There's a whole other world that can only be reached by delving into the power of the mind and the various regions of the unconscious where the potential is unlimited.

Victoria: And one more place, the power of the heart, the realm of love.

(Paul gets up and walks around, mumbling to himself as he thinks.)

Paul: *(looking at Harry)* The power of the mind has it's appeal.

            (walking over to Victoria) And the power of the heart is definitely worth considering.

> *(thinking a moment)* Both are interesting concepts if they could potentially lead somewhere. However, *(pointing over his shoulder towards Jon)* I can do without the power of the fruitcake.

(Stage door right opens and Boris enters wearing a white researcher's coat and carrying a briefcase. He sits down at a table at stage right and places the briefcase on the table in front of him. He opens it and we see that it is a laptop computer. He begins punching away at the keyboard.)

Harry: Hmmm, what do we have here?

Victoria: We think the two of you should be able to handle this one without us.

(Paul and Harry converge on the man with the computer.)

Paul: Hello, I'm Paul Satin, and this is Harry Hood.

(Man looks up without responding, nods to them and goes back to the computer.)

Harry: Interesting contraption you got there. Does it tell the time?

Boris: This is the SF 6900. It's capable of expropriating the total knowledge of humankind on several microchips for easy storage. It's problem solving potential is unlimited.

Harry: Impressive.

Paul   Amazing.

Boris: The SF 6900 represents the latest technology in the ever progressive advancement of the human race.

Harry: Can it make an elephant disappear?

Boris: Uhh, no, of course not, but with the right database I could compute the necessary requirements to produce a beam of intense heat the would disintegrate the elephant down to a few microbes within seconds.

Harry: I was making a joke.

Boris: *(smiles)* Of course.

Paul: Excuse me, but you've peaked my interest in this little gizmo. You say this machine holds the entire knowledge of humankind?

Boris: Yes, that's right.

Paul: And that by punching a few of those buttons you can summon up all that knowledge to read on that small screen?

Boris: *(proudly)* Yes.

Paul: And that by punching in a few other buttons you can use all this knowledge to work on and solve any problem that you ask it?

Boris: Almost anything.

Paul: Almost anything, or anything?

Boris: Well, er. . . . yes! Anything.

Paul: Can it answer a simple question for me?

Boris: The SF 6900 has been designed to solve any problem that is asked of it. Its potential in mechanical and scientific research is greater than the collective minds of Galileo, Einstein, Newton, DaVinci and Hawking.

Paul: Why are we here?

Boris: (ignoring Paul's question) For example, if you wanted to determine the amount of molecules in any given cubic foot of space, I could feed the information into the SF 6900 and obtain sufficient data to analyze . . .

Paul: Why are we here?

Boris: . . . the exact amount of air in any given area. Then by taking the mean of the average we could . . .

Paul: (grabbing his arm) Why are we here?

Harry: Take it easy Paul, you don't want to unbalance a scientifically balanced mind.

Boris: (to Paul) Pardon?

Paul: Listen carefully. Why . . . are . . . we . . . here?

Boris: That's your question?

Paul: That's my question.

Boris: Well, that's going to take a little time. The computations necessary to equate this problem are lengthy and complex. There will be a lot of information that I'll have to enter manually and it'll take some time before I'll be able to analyse the final results.

Paul: Okay, then why don't you get started. Don't be afraid to ask if you need any help.

Boris: I'm sure that the SF 6900 and I will be able to handle the problem.

Sally: Would you like anything from the bar first.

Boris: Yes indeed, I would like a . . .

Paul: We can have a toast after you've solved the problem. I don't want any wrong answers because the technician put his plug in the wrong outlet.

Victoria: He won't be able to help you. *(they all turn to look at Victoria)* We've have dealt with his kind before. They know all the answers and what they don't know they will eventually find out. Scientists, researchers, mathematicians, they know everything. Everything except what you really want to know.

Boris: Excuse me madam, but if you're referring to the question that Mr. Satin has asked, I'm sure that within a reasonable scope of time I'll be able to reach a hypothesis that . . . .

Victoria: *(standing quickly, visually upset)* Hypothesis! We already have enough damned hypotheses. Another will not make any difference.

Boris: But madam, you must begin with a hypothesis. To solve any problem there is a logical order for solution. A fine example is the theory of evolving life-forms. It began with a hypothesis and through the years we've been able to reach certain conclusions through hard research about our ancestral beginnings.

Victoria: Are you referring to the biological accident theories?

Boris: I wouldn't put it quite that way, but in essence, yes.

Victoria: *(looking sternly at him)* WE are not a biological accident.

Boris: But we've been able to isolate and develop a
            molecular ratio to produce a possible . . .

Victoria: When We look into your eyes We see
            something, something that tells us you're a
            thinking human being and not a stuffed animal
            in a museum. Call it a spirit, call it a soul, call it
            a life energy force, or call it whatever you like,
            and We know that one living being can identify
            that essence within another.

            Science can research the physical body, how it
            works and what it's composed of. Scientists can
            tell you exactly how many billions of cells there
            are, but they can not tell you why each one of
            those fragile cells continues to exist, why they
            survive, why they reproduce or why a few
            trillion of them have inter-connected to create
            that special entity called a human being.

            But there are two things that science cannot
            explain, thought and love.

            Everything else in the universe has a scientific
            formula, or eventually will.

            Everything else can be dissected, analyzed,
            tested, inspected, mathematically formulated
            and technically redrawn . . . except for thought
            and love.

Boris: Through science, we have been able to identify
            cell structures within the DNA that can be
            traced back to their primordial origins.

Victoria: The scientists can identify the form, they can
            identify the shape and they can identify the
            substance, but scientists cannot identify or
            explain the essence.

Boris: But through science we can . . . .

Victoria: *(cutting off Boris)* A million years from now your
            science and technology will be able to solve
            every complicated problem in the universe, but
            because of their complexity, they'll never be
            able to answer the simplest of questions.
            Where did we come from, why are we here, and
            where do we go.

(Victoria turns away from Boris. Paul moves next to her.)

Paul: Victoria, may I hold your hand in mine.

Victoria: Why?

Paul: I want to feel that passion that is so deep within
            you. I want to hold a little bit of the essence
            that gives your will such strength.

*(Victoria slowly turns towards Paul and shyly smiles, and
then extends her hand. Paul holds her hand with both
of his.)*

Paul: You truly are something special. There is a
            grace within you that brings a calmness to my
            life with just your presence . . . I'm just finding it
            hard to understand this ethereal stuff. I mean,
            look at Jon.

Victoria: Jon is a megalomaniac. He believes in a
            religion that only makes him important. We
            believe in a religious equality for all. *(with
            emphasis on the "I")* I believe in the power of
            the heart, the power of love.

Boris: The biological accident theory is a rational,
            logical explanation. It has a basis for equation.
            The theory of the Supreme Being has no
            practical basis anywhere.

(Letting go of Paul's hand.)

Victoria: When the early caveman buried their tribesmen with food and weapons, preparing them for the afterlife, how did they know there was one?

Boris: Perhaps it was their only explanation to justify their primitive existence on earth.

Victoria: What you consider to be primitive human beings on some evolutionary path, already had the ability for abstract thought and a sense of the divine.

Boris: Yes, but once abstract concepts began to develop within human thought patterns, wouldn't the reason for living be one of the first questions.

Victoria: Using your methods of evolutionary thinking, it would be irrational to believe that these early humans could have had the basis for such reflective abstact thought.

Boris: The development of abstact thought coincided with the general evolution of the primitives within their environment.

   The idea of a Supreme Being may have been invented as part of the evolutionary process. The human mind had developed to the point of becoming a sentient consciousness with questions that went beyond pure survival, questions that looked for meaning and could not find any. It became a consciousness on the verge of madness, so it developed an omni-present being with mysterious intentions in order to allow the mind to further grow without having to face the madness of reality.

Victoria: Scientists have speculated that these primitives learned everything from basic trial and error. They hid from the animals until they figured out how to use the wood and stone for weapons. Then it took many more years before they began reshaping those raw materials for tools.

These primitives painted hunters and animals on the walls of caves because they only painted what they could see. They didn't paint abstract thoughts.

Now We ask you, how could these primitive human beings, who took years to figure out how to use the tools lying in front of them, who could only be taught that fire was hot by getting burnt, who only believed in what they could see, how could these primitives come up with such an abstract thought as an afterlife?

The idea of a Supreme Being or an afterlife should have been totally incomprehensible to them. Their thoughts encompassed their basic needs, their survival. When you can tell us why they buried their dead in preparation for an afterlife, then we'll listen to your machine.

(Victoria turns and walks back to her chair and sits. There is a slight pause of silence.)

Harry: Bravo! Bravo!

(Sally and Jon cheer along with Harry. Paul and Boris remain silent.)

Jon: That's right Victoria, you tell him. Science is not the way to paradise. I am.

Paul: Stuff it Jon *(then turning to Boris)* and you get started.

Jon: Forget him Paul, follow me. I'll show you the answers, all of you. Together through my guidance we can live in eternal bliss, loving one another for all eternity in my own Pub.

(Doorman bursts in through stage door left.)

Doorman: James, Jon James.

Jon: *(calmly)* No, I'm not going.

Doorman: *(taken slightly aback)* Mr. James?

Jon: I'll decide when I want to leave.

Doorman: Mr. James, there is no choice in the matter, you must come now.

Jon: Ha! You can't call me. Do you know who I am? I'm Jon James. I make my own decisions.

Doorman: Please now Mr. James, don't make any trouble.

Jon: I'm going to open my own Pub where everyone will love me and do as I say.

          Who's going to join me. I'll lead you to paradise. I will be Zeus and you can all be Gods with me on Mount Olympus. Come with me Paul and all your questions will be answered. Victoria, join me, I'll take care of you. I'll make you my queen, we'll rule our own pub. Come everyone, come . . . .

(The Doorman takes a handgun from his coat and shoots Jon in the back. Jon falls to the ground.)

Doorman: Come now Mr. James, come quietly now.

(Jon stirs, then gets up from the floor and dusts of his pants, straightens his clothes and walks out with his head bowed low, avoiding the stare of the others who remain in shocked silence.)

Paul: Holy Shit.

Harry: You can say that again.

Boris: Actually there's never been proof of any substance that's been excreted by a divine being. Only animals, fish and some insects produce a biodegradable expulsion of natural . . .

Paul: Have you got the answer to my question?

Boris: Err, no.

Paul: Then please, get started.

(Lights dim, curtain closes.)

Act Two – Scene One

(The lights go on onstage but the curtain remains closed. From behind the curtain, audience hears actor Jake Javelin quoting Shakespeare and the others in the bar applauding. Jake overacts all his lines.)

Jake: To be or not to be, that is the question. (Hamlet)

(the others applaud)

It is silliness to live when to live is torment: and then we have a prescription to die when death is our physician. (Othello)

(others applaud, the curtain opens)

All the world's a stage, And all the men and women merely players: They have their exits and their entrances. And one man in his time plays many parts. (As You Like It)

(others applaud)

Honest company, I thank you all. That have beheld me give away myself. (Taming of the Shrew)

(Jake goes to the bar and orders drinks for everyone.)

A toast to you all for your time and pleasure. I would give all my fame for a pot of ale and safety. (Henry V)

Sally: *(expressing the following toasts as she pours drinks)*

If you know the truth, they label you as crazy.

If your spiritual beliefs differ from the mainstream, they call you unbalanced.

If you question the accepted reality of the society in which you live, you are classified as mentally unstable.

If you take action against the lies and deceit of the world order, then you are branded as an anarchist.

If you protest the indifference of the privileged, you are a public menace.

(Everyone mills around while the drinks are being poured, then take their drinks and return to their respective places. Jake remains at the bar with the Sally. Paul, Harry and Victoria return to their seats, Boris returns to his machine.)

Jake: The fool doth think he is wise, but the wise man knows himself to be a fool. (As You Like It)

Sally: Shut up Jake, the shows over.

(Stage door right opens. Enter Eric wearing dark glasses and carrying a white cane. Victoria gets up right away to guide him.)

Victoria: Here let us help you.

Eric: *(with a slightly timid sound to his voice)* Thank you very much.

Victoria: *(taking him by his left elbow to act as a guide)* Why don't you come sit with us.

Eric: *(resisting)* Oh, I don't know, I'm not very good company.

Victoria: Why not?

Eric: Well I'm not very good at talking and I get very uncomfortable when people are charitable towards me.

Harry: Never you mind, you come right here and sit with us, we'll be more than pleased to have you share our time.

(Victoria leads him to a chair next to Paul who gets up and moves away from Eric. Victoria and Harry look questioningly at Paul. Paul makes a hand motion that he doesn't want to be near Eric.)

Eric: Thank you, you are most kind. My name is Eric.

Victoria: We are Victoria, this is Harry.

Harry: Hello.

Eric: Hello Harry and Victoria and Victoria.

Victoria: *(grabbing Paul's arm, forcing him back as he is about to leave)* And this is Paul.

Paul: Yeah, hi.

Eric: I'm very pleased to meet you all. Please don't let me interrupt your conversation. If I may, I'll just sit here. I like to listen.

Paul: Well excuse me, I've got some work to do.

Victoria: *(a bit sternly)* Paul.

Eric: Please don't let me interrupt. I'm sorry if my character in this pantomime has caused you any bother.

Paul: Oh no, no problem at all. I just have a few things I've got to do.

(Paul walks over to Boris who is working on the machine.)

Victoria: Eric, We are very sorry. We want to apologize for his indifference.

Eric: It's quite alright. I'm accustomed to it.

Harry: Can I get you a drink or something.

Eric: Oh, no, thank you. I never consume spirits, they tend to make me act funny.

Victoria: They make everyone act funny, each of us in different ways.

Eric: For me, alcohol tends to make me aggressive and bold.

Harry: That's how many people act when they're sober.

Jake: This above all: to thine own self be true. (Hamlet)

Eric: Please don't get me wrong. I guess what I mean to say is that it gives me a sense of courage. I do foolish things like insult people who are rude, or criticize others for their bad manners. When I drink alcohol it fools me into acting as if I were an equal among them.

Harry: *(Sympathetically)* Eric, everyone is equal, we all have the same rights and freedoms as any other human.

Eric: Yes, in essence you are right, but, I am a person with limited abilities, and when I drink I tend to forget this.

Victoria: Eric, you can't live your life feeling less of a person than others.

Eric: Why not?

Victoria: Because it just isn't right.

Eric: Most people treat me with kindness and respect as long I keep portraying what they think a limited person should be like. Too much alcohol makes me forget my limitations. Once I'm sober again, I am myself once more but the damage I've caused while drinking remains.

Victoria: Eric, We . . . I feel so sad.

Eric: That's because you're a person of the heart.

(Victoria and Harry look at Eric.)

Eric: Did I say something wrong?

Victoria: No, actually you're quite right, but how did you know.

Eric: I'm not sure. Sometimes I just know something to be true. It's like an instinct, I may meet someone and know exactly the type of person they are, even if they try to hide it. Sometimes I'm even able to predict things like the outcome of a sporting event or a moment of historical clarity. However, when I consciously attempt to predict something, I'm always wrong, so I've learned to just allow it to happen, like learning to listen to an inner voice.

Harry: A Savant.

Victoria: A what?

Harry: A Savant. A psychological term used to describe somebody who shows a specialized talent, like the ability for instant mathematical calculation or an extraordinary memory for dates and facts.

Paul: *(to Boris)* Can you explain it in layman's language so that I can understand.

Boris: Well . . . science requires mathematical thinking, a process that comes naturally to humans as it is the basis of much of our interaction with others. Counting money, making change, calculating interests and so on.

Paul: Yes, but why is it taking so long to come up with an answer?

Boris: The computations are copiously complicated with cryptic complexity.

Sally: Wow, that sounded like poetry.

Paul: Sounds more like science fiction.

Jake: Oft, expectation fails, and most oft where most it promises. (All's Well That Ends Well)

(Stage door right opens, a man wearing a monks robe enters the Pub and walks to the centre stage with his head bowed as if he was praying, a hood covers his head.)

Sally: Oh, oh, looks like trouble.

Boris: Could be another religious cult, I've seen them before, some of them are very controversial.

Paul: A religious cult?

Boris: Yes, they spring up every so often, praising one thing or another. Nothing they believe in is based on fact, just legends and myths.

(Paul gets up and proceeds to survey the monk. He casually walks around him in a circle, eventually sticking his head under the bowed hood looking at the monk face to face.)

Paul: Hello there.

Monk: Blessings be with you sir.

Paul: I was just wondering if you were looking for directions or if you were just looking.

Monk: I no longer need to search. I have found the answer.

Paul: Maybe you would like to share it with us.

Monk: *(pulling back his hood for all to see. He is the same actor who played Jon James.)* All truth lies with the Supreme Being. He is the one, the only one.

Paul: Are you talking about the Proprietor?

Monk: It does not matter by what name you call Him, as long as you recognize that He is the truth that embodies all things.

Sally: Unless it turns out to be a Her.

Paul: *(turning to Harry)* Harry, doesn't this guy look familiar to you. Like another Zealot that was here a while back preaching about the Supreme Being.

Harry: Yes, a striking resemblance.

Paul: You know brother, you look just like another character we had in here. His name was Jon James.

Monk: I am a monk in the order of the followers of the prophet Jon James.

Paul: The prophet! Are you kidding.

Monk: I'm sorry sir, but it would be sacrilege to jest
          about Prophet Jon, bless his wholesome soul.
          He was an inspiration and an example, sent to
          instruct us on the true way, the road to
          paradise.

Paul: You're as crazy as he was.

Monk: Sir, you may not be a believer but there is no
          call to insult and persecute. I only wish to
          follow the example of the Prophet Jon.

Paul: That's what I'm afraid of. When did all this
          Prophet Jon idiocracy start?

Monk: Immediately after his martyrdom.

Harry: His martyrdom?

Monk: *(turning to Harry)* Yes, after he was killed by the
          pagans, his word was carried by his followers.
          His love for all people and his passion to
          achieve paradise for everyone has comforted
          many lost souls.

Harry: I'm curious, how was he killed?

Monk: Tied to a chair, he was pierced with flaming
          spears while he prayed his devotion to the
          Supreme Being. It was a true portrait of love
          and courage, he showed no fear of death.

Paul: *(laughing)* I hate to disappoint a misguided
          monk, but your prophet was a raging
          egomaniac who craved to hold power over his
          own private little world.

Monk: *(turning fiercely on Paul)* Blasphemer! May the
          Supreme Being slit your tongue with blades of
          fire.

Paul:	*(still laughing)* Listen you hooded zombie, I knew your Prophet Jon personally and he was no saint or prophet.
Monk:	Liar! Blasphemer! Liar! You've been sent by the evil one to tempt me. The Prophet Jon said that we are sent here to be tested and you are proof of this. Begone messenger of evil, hold back your powers of coercion and seek not to test me. *(he turns and walks to the other end of the bar)*
Sally:	Would you like a drink?
Monk:	I abhor alcohol.
Sally:	I ain't no whore. I might be aggressively promiscuous but that's because I explore all parts of my sensual nature.
Monk:	Woman, you are a servant of the evil one. *(Monk turns from the bar and walks away)*
Paul:	I don't believe this.
Harry:	What's not to believe.
Paul:	Everything! It's all absurd. We're stuck in this Pub not knowing where we come from or where we are going or even why we're here. Now we've got another weirdo who spews stories about prophets and Supreme Beings.
Harry:	I understand how some people could succumb very easily to characters like Jon James.
Paul:	You mean other loonies.
Harry:	No, I mean rational intelligent people who are also looking for answers.

Paul: But how can anyone follow a lunatic like Jon
           James.

Harry: Most times it's the intensity of the individual
           that seems to give credence to their words.
           They believe with such conviction that others
           see whatever answer they present as the truth.
           Many people have been searching so long and
           have become so frustrated that they are willing
           to accept any answer presented to them. It's
           not surprising that people fall under the
           influence of someone like Jon James. He
           offers paradise and people accept it.

Paul: Are you trying to tell me that Jon James could
           be right.

Harry: No, but I will say that I'm not sure if he was
           totally wrong.

Paul: You're suggesting that there is a Supreme
           Being.

Harry: There are countless possibilities. The theory
           of a Supreme Being is one, even though I
           personally don't believe in Him, or Her, or
           whatever it's supposed to be. I believe that
           there is something but I don't follow the
           traditional concepts of a Supreme Being.

Paul: That's what I like about you Harry, you're very
           definite about your non-commitment.

Harry: It's rather hard to explain. I'm not even sure
           if I can formalize it in my own mind, but
           somewhere in the past I made spiritual contact.

Victoria: You made contact? We would like to hear this.

Eric: Yes, please tell us. I would like to hear it as well as Victoria and Victoria.

Harry: Alright, if you wish. Once I was standing amidst the circle of the ancient Stonehenge monoliths. I felt something, like the mystical essence or force. I turned slowly in the circle and saw an old man. Somehow I knew that he was a guardian of the ages.

            He stood before me, not saying anything, but I knew from his warm smile that he accepted my presence. I spoke and asked him to tell me the knowledge and secrets of the ancient ones. He just smiled, but I understood his silent message. I understood that I wasn't ready yet, and that I must continue searching and exploring, and maybe in this life, or maybe in another dimension, I would one day find the answer. Then my memory fades and that's all I can remember.

Paul: Nice story Harry, but to me that's all it is, a story. Maybe it was an insight into your life but it's not an insight to mine.

Harry: I don't know. Perhaps it was a dream, or my subconscious mind trying to reach out to me. Maybe I'll just end up like Jon with illusions of grandeur.

Victoria: No Harry, you won't end up like Jon.

Eric: Who's Jon?

Paul: A very weird and disturbed person.

Eric: Why do you think of him like that?

Paul: He had this bizarre idea of opening his own Pub and having everyone love him.

Eric: What's wrong with wanting to be loved?

Paul: There's nothing wrong with love Eric, it can be a delightful feeling, I just don't believe that it has ever really solved anything.

Victoria: No Paul, you're wrong, love can solve most things.

Eric: I may be blind and limited, but I know how to love. I know I'm not handsome or desirable but there are people who love me, and I can recognize that love, and return love to them.

Paul: That may be fine for you Eric but the rest of us need more substance.

Victoria: Paul!

Paul: Well I'm sorry Vic but listening to crazy monks and savants is not my idea of finding the answer. I admit that love is wonderful, that you are wonderful, but I don't think that love is the answer to my question.

Victoria: Dammit Paul, do you even know what you're looking for?

Paul: You're right, damned bloody right! And that's the whole damned problem and it's gonna eat me up inside until there ain't anything left inside of me that's worth looking for.

Jake: Doubt that the sun doth move, doubt truth to be a liar, but never doubt I love. (Hamlet)

Harry: Why turn down all possibilities without exploring them.

Paul: How can I explore something that's an unsubstantial feeling.

Victoria: By experience.

Paul: How I can experience something when I'm not even sure that it's there.

Victoria: It is hard to find because we don't always know what to call it. Some call it the truth and others call it the meaning of life. We call it love, but We don't know how to define or explain it. All we know is that once we have found it, then knowing what to call it no longer seems to matter.

Paul: It matters to me Victoria, it matters to me. Where do I look? Here, in this broken down old Pub. (shyly) So far, the only truly meaningful thing I have found is you.

Victoria: Paul, it's not something that you find and wear like a diamond. It's something that you have to choose and make happen. Even though the choices are usually difficult, look deep in your heart, and you will know just what they are. Maybe it's because you're not really looking.

Paul: What do you mean?

Victoria: All you're doing is arguing against whatever anyone else has found. Some have found their own answers which you can't accept because it is their answer and not meant for you, therefore you persecute them because it is not what you want.

Paul: I'd be happy to accept their answers if they could only give me some proof.

Victoria: What kind of proof do you need?

Paul: Something more substantial than theory and conjecture.

Victoria: Paul, we're talking about the human potential to touch the divine. We're talking about the ability to feel the deepest connection with another person. I'm talking about love.

Boris: How do you know it's real and not some part of the evolutionary process of intelligence. How can you measure it?

Victoria: Measure! Measure what, the ineffable!

             I have stood in front of paintings that made me melt.

             I've seen statues that held me in such awe that tears rolled down my face.

             I've read poems that have lifted me beyond my mundane existence.

             I've seen moving pictures that inspired me to be more than human.

             I've heard music that brought me into the realm of angels, and brought me into the trance of devils.

             I've read books that shattered my heart and others that took my soul to dimensions elevated beyond my wildest dreams.

(All stop and stare at Victoria. She looks around, gets a bit shy, then composes.)

             The incredible love you feel at the birth of your child.

> The devastating sorrow that ruptures your heart when your most precious love is lost.

(Turns to Boris.)

> The intensity of all these feelings are not the result of a chemical reaction or an electrical current within the synapses of the brain. Love is not an accident of the evolutionary process.

(She stops, looks around and shyly looks down at her drink.)

Paul: Victoria, if I sound hard, I don't mean to be, especially not with you. Eric, I'm sorry, the last thing I would want to do is to hurt you, any of you. It's just that I've got to know why I'm here and find a purpose for myself.

Victoria: We know and We want to help.

Paul: Talk to me Victoria, what is it that makes you so strong and confident and yet so gentle and calm.

Victoria: We don't know the words you want to hear. All We know is the thoughts in our mind, and the feelings in our heart.

Paul: *(tenderly)* Tell me your thoughts, please.

Victoria: *(emphasis on the "I")* I believe in a higher power but I cannot offer any proof. I can't fill your emptiness with the truth because I don't know what the truth is. I've accepted that in my life.

> What I know to be real is love. It has the grace and the power to make all those negative feelings and thoughts dissipate like the morning mist at sunrise.

Paul: Maybe I'm like those primitives you spoke of.
            I have to see with my own eyes and I just can't
            accept a benevolent being that plops us down
            into the middle of nothing for no reason.

            And yet, with my own eyes, I see the grace that
            is so deep within you.

Boris: Ah, excuse me Mr. Satin. *(pauses for a moment
            when Paul doesn't respond)* Excuse me, Paul.

Paul: Yes, what is it.

Boris: The SF 6900 has come up with an answer to
            your question.

*(Paul stands up quickly, Victoria and Harry sit upright in
shock. All the others in the bar turn towards Boris, wide
eyed. Paul crosses to where Boris is sitting. Boris hands
him a piece of paper. Paul reads it to himself.)*

Paul: I don't understand.

Harry: What does it say.

Paul: Ex nihilo nihil fit.

Harry: Well, that explains everything of course.

Paul: *(to Boris)* Is this some sort of computer code?

Boris: No, I . . . ah . . . I'm as confused as you are. It's
            not any basic programming language that I'm
            aware of. I don't have any idea what it could
            mean.

Paul: Then what are we supposed to do with this.

Victoria: Perhaps its an anagram of some sort, read it
            back to us.

Paul: Ex nihilo nihil fit.

Eric: It's Latin.

(They all turn to look at Eric.)

Victoria: Eric, you understand Latin.

Eric: Yes, my mother used to read it to me when
          I was a child. She would sit by my bed and
          read it to help me fall asleep.

Paul: What does it mean?

Eric: It means "Out of nothing, nothing comes."

Paul: Out of nothing, nothing comes. What's the
          machine trying to say?

Boris: Maybe it's trying to tell us that there is nothing
          out there, that this is all there is and that we are
          basically nothing.

Victoria: We will not accept that.

Monk: The machine is a tool of the evil one trying to
          poison your mind.

Jake: The devil can cite Scripture for his purpose.
          (The Merchant of Venice)

Harry: I agree with Victoria, the answer is totally
          unacceptable to all of my reasoning and
          experience.

Boris: But what else could it mean? I think it's rather
          obvious according to the question Mr. Satin
          asked.

Sally: It's got to be a mistake because I was
          personally hired by the Proprietor's assistant to
          run this bar.

Paul: But a machine can't lie. Perhaps its wrong, maybe you punched a wrong button somewhere when entering the data.

Boris: There is no mistake. I've run the program three times to check it and came up with the same answer each time.

Paul: But it doesn't make any sense. We're here, we're real, we're something. The machine can't be right.

Eric: Out of nothing, nothing comes. The machine is correct, it is the truth.

(They all turn again to stare at Eric.)

Paul: Go on.

Eric: The machine is trying to tell us that it can't answer your question. It is the machine that is nothing and therefore can give you nothing. It can't explain life because it has never experienced life itself.

(There's a long pause where no one says anything.)

Eric: Did I say anything wrong?

Victoria: No Eric, you said something very right.

Harry: Thank you Eric, your insight has the purity of innocence.

Paul: However, that leaves us back at the beginning. No answers, no clues, just speculation and frustration.

Boris: And the theory of the Big Biological Accident.

Monk: And faith in the Supreme Being.

Victoria: And with Love.

(Stage door left opens and the Doorman bursts in.)

Doorman: Javelin . . . Jake Javelin.

Jake: Out, out, brief candle! Life is but a walking shadow, a poor player that struts and frets his hour upon the stage and then is heard no more: it is a tale told by an idiot, full of sound and fury, signifying nothing. (MacBeth)

(Everyone pauses for a moment and returns to their chairs that they had before, except Boris who remains standing.)

Boris: Mr. Satin.

Paul: Yeah.

Boris: Are there any other projects you want me to research?

Paul: I don't know, why ask me?

Boris: Well, I'm a scientist. I search for truth through logical research and study. I do not believe that some supernatural entity would give us the gift of sense and reason along with a sentient intellect just so that we can decline to use them.

Paul: Do whatever you wanna do. It's your life.

Boris: Perhaps I could investigate some more answers for you.

Paul: Listen, why don't you research something for somebody else. Find a new martini recipe for the Barmaid.

Harry: *(to Boris)* That little machine you got there, could I ask you a question about it.

Boris: Yes.

Harry: Do you think you could run some calculations on the size of a human brain and the capacity that it will contain.

Boris: I could compute the mean average of brain size and then compare with known cases of people who were of extraordinary intelligence.

Harry: Yeah, that might work.

Eric: If you don't mind my prying, may I ask why?

Harry: Well Eric, I have a theory about why some people are more or less gifted than others. I believe that it is something mystical and I want to explore the capabilities of the human brain. Maybe some people are gifted because there is a facet of their brain that acts as a receptacle for extraordinary powers.

Eric: I'm not sure I understand.

Paul: Neither do I.

Harry: I have always been fascinated with the way certain individuals throughout history have been able to do things that the average person could not, and I would like to explore the reasons why.

          Mozart was a brilliant pianist at the age of five, wrote his first symphony at the age of seven and created all those masterpieces before dying at the age of thirty-two. And yet other people, even if they practiced for fifty years, could never be able to play the piano as well as Mozart did when he was five.

Boris: It's been well documented that Mozart was a result of parental pressure and expectations forced upon him by his father.

Harry: Partially true, but if my father had pushed me the way Mozart's father had, I know that I would not have mastered music anywhere near as well as Mozart, it's just not in me. But on the other hand, perhaps Mozart's father urged his son only after recognizing the ability that was already there.

Paul: Perhaps the kid was a mutant created by an imbalance of brain chemistry.

Harry: That's possible, but then he was not unique because there are many cases throughout history where people have had special talents that others have not.

Boris: Like Einstein, Galileo and DaVinci.

Harry: Exactly.

Paul: But couldn't they have learned through their environment.

Harry: Yes, but something had to be there to begin with.

Paul: Are we not all empty in the beginning, a blank slate, and everything is injected into us by our parents, friends and what we learn from experience.

Harry: I can't buy that, it doesn't explain all the unknown answers.

Paul: I think it does, we learn everything, and that is why no two people are alike, because no two people ever grow up in the exact same circumstances.

Victoria: What about love?

Paul: *(smiling shyly)* What about it?

Victoria: You can't teach love, it is something you have to feel.

Paul: A child learns love from its parents. It learns from the example given by them.

Victoria: Some children grow up without parents, or some have parents that are unloving, yet when the time comes, that child still knows what love is. If it wasn't something you were born to need then how could you suffer from its absence.

(Paul makes to object but Victoria cuts him off.)

I don't mean sex. I mean love, real love, the kind of love that you would die for. Have you ever loved anyone that much Paul?

Have you ever loved someone so much that it fills every essence of your being, so much that it could turn you into a hollow ghost of yourself when they're gone.

You can't teach that to anyone.

Paul: Victoria, until I met you I had never felt that way towards anyone.

Victoria: Love Paul, real love.

Never mind what the others think. Never mind what you're supposed to do in life. When you find real love, nothing else matters. It doesn't even matter if your life was predestined for you.

Even if you're as lonely as a monarch.

Paul: Victoria, I think that will always have this burning need to find a reason for my existence, but now, here with you, that need to know is fading to the background of my mind. More and more I find my thoughts are of you.

Is this love Vic? Is this what you feel? Does your heart touch mine?

Victoria: In the end, it's only the love that matters, for any measure of life rises or falls with the power of love. When love is full, then both the intellect and the soul rest in its contentment. It can fill up so much of the emptiness. It can answer so many of your questions.

Paul: *(reacting as if he had a revelation)* I've been trying so hard to find some abstract answer, I never realized that the answer might be you.

Victoria: That's what real love can do.

Paul: Victoria, I'm afraid. I'm afraid that I may have wasted so much time looking for meaning and not seeing it.

Victoria: Love gives life meaning.

Paul: Yes, I realize that now, when you're with me . . . I have meaning.

(Stage door left opens and the Doorman bursts in.)

Doorman: King, Victoria King.

Paul: NO!!!

(Paul makes for the Doorman, but the Doorman holds up his hand and freezes Paul in time. Victoria walks up to Paul and kisses him on the cheek.)

Victoria: Goodbye Paul.

(She begins to walk out, just before she leaves, she stops and turns and speaks.)

Victoria: Paul, if anyone ever tries to tell you that you can't love someone too much, it's because they have never tried.

(Victoria leaves. The Doorman looks at Paul for a couple of seconds and then closes the door behind him. Paul picks up a chair and throws it across the room towards the door, then turns away, hands to his face.)

Act Two – Scene Two

(Harry, Paul and Eric sit at a table at the front of the stage, Boris at the computer, Monk sitting alone, Fred standing at the bar, Elvis and Sally behind the bar out of sight.)

Eric: You never realize how important love is until a few moments after it's gone. Then with time you forget and make the same mistakes all over again. Perhaps its fate.

Harry: I don't believe in fate. Our lives are not pre-determined.

Paul: *(solemnly)* Why?

Harry: That would mean that we're not free.

Paul: And you call this freedom? Trapped in this pub until our names are called. Watching the people you love taken from you with no warning, for no reason.

Harry: In a physical sense yes, we are trapped within these containers we call our bodies. But we are spiritually and intellectually free, we can believe and think whatever we want. We can accept ideas or reject them as is our fancy.

Paul: What about brainwashed zombies like the monk.

Harry: He still controls his own mind, however it has been focused to think in a particular direction.

Boris: Then he is not free. He is like my computer, programmed in his functionality.

Harry: With determination he can free himself on his
            own accord, as can we all. That is our real
            power, our freedom. We have the capability
            to resist the alluring temptation of societies
            illusions, and shape our minds in our own
            ideals.

Monk: Or create our own illusions.

*(The Monk walks to the center of the stage, looks up at
the audience for a few moments, a look of determined
enlightenment, then turns and walks to stand in front of
the stage left door.)*

(Stage door left opens and The Doorman bursts in.)

Doorman: Smith . . . *(surprised a little that the Monk is
            there waiting)*

            John Smith.

(The Monk bows his head, then walks out in silence.)

Harry: Wow, I wasn't expecting that.

Paul: Do you think he knew, or was that a lucky
            guess.

Boris: No, I think somehow he knew. He knew of the
            forces that go beyond my calculations.
            Everything I research is a set of natural laws and
            equations, and yet I cannot find the source as
            to why these laws and equations even exist.

Paul: Maybe you're free Harry, but I'm not. I'm a
            prisoner to my own ignorance.

Harry: You've built your own prison. You can only
            escape by breaking down the walls that you
            yourself erected.

Fred: You guys are pathetic.

(They all turn to look at Fred.)

Boris: I beg your pardon. Although partially accurate, that's a rather general analysis of what is only a sub-section of this study group.

Fred: Listen to yourselves. You've been moaning about the loss of a loved one and then segue into a jailbreak out of your own self inflicted dungeons. You've polarized your emotions in an obvious attempt to avoid the grief that you feel.

Harry: As intelligent beings we are trying to delve into the realms of human consciousness.

Fred: *(sarcastically)* In your dreams. People don't really want freedom because then they would have to accept responsibility for their lives and their actions.

In my studies I have found that people would rather have a scapegoat to blame all their problems and failures on . . . like a divine master or supreme beings, something other-worldly so that they can point their finger at the sky and say "His fault, Her fault, Their fault."

Paul: And what if we're just seeking the truth.

Fred: From foibles to failures to scientific fallacies, one looks everywhere for the truth.

Boris: I seek truth through the scientific study of reality, of nature and the cosmos.

Fred: Science can be a debatable illusion, but science cannot give us the answer to everything.

Measuring the distance between you and I, identifying the molecules that float between us and understanding the effect of the photons emitted from the lights above will not answer your primal questions.

Boris: Would you recognize the truth? And would your truth be nothing more than the quantum probability of many truths.

Fred: Perhaps our illusion is to believe that we can attain the answers that science cannot provide.

Boris: There is no illusion with science. There is the flash of insight which is then developed into an hypothesis that is never fully accepted until proven through repeated testing, intense scrutiny and clinical examination.

Only after all doubt is removed we have fact, which we can then translate into the universal encrypted laws of nature.

Fred: Your statement has merit, for in the long run, nothing can withstand logic and reason, but there will always be doubt, and while there is doubt, we think. Perhaps that is the purpose of doubt, for if there was no doubt, would we stop thinking?

Boris: Reality has to be accepted for what it is, not what you want it to be.

Fred: Don't all of the varied sciences and religions provide systems of truth based illusions that feign as wishful reality?

Paul: (sarcastically) Whew, listen to the fancy talker. Where'd you get your degree in analysis for psychos.

Eric: Paul, I think he might be right.

Paul: I know, he probably is right, and that's what
            pisses me off.

Eric: Sorry.

Paul: No Eric, I'm the one that's sorry. I just seem to
            keep banging my head against invisible walls.

Fred: The problem as I see it, is that you are trying to
            find answers to multi-dimensional questions
            with one-dimensional logic and practical
            science.

            Instead of trying to follow the complicated
            mind mazes that you create, start at one point
            and follow a straight line to its end.

*(Paul straightens as if struck by a jolt, then proceeds to and
enters the toilet.)*

Boris: It is our ability to research and systematically
            investigate everything we observe or feel, smell
            and think, that elevates us as a species.
            Otherwise we are nothing more than evolved
            monkeys inhabiting an insignificant giant rock.

            And yet, we are able to contemplate the
            universe. That must make us special.

Fred: Sir, you are obviously a man of practical logic
            and precise reason, and those are qualities that
            I hold dear, for I do not disagree with anything
            you have said. However, I often see the
            impractical in our actions and the unreasonable
            in our explanations.

Paul: *(emerging from the toilet with a rush and with
            sudden enthusiasm)* Simplicity! The straight
            line! Hey buddy, what's your name?

Fred: Fred . . . . my name is Fred.

Paul: Fred, you're a genius.

Fred: Why thank you for the compliment. May I use it in my resume?

Paul: You've given me an insight to a potential solution.

Fred: Maybe I should take up counseling as a practice. What is the solution if you don't mind my asking?

Paul: If the answers are ineffable and hidden in mystery, then start with the obvious.

Fred: Whenever I want to explore the ineffable, I write poetry.

Paul: It's the straight line you said, simply follow the yellow brick road.

Eric: I don't think it's that easy Paul.

Paul: Harry, it's obvious.

Harry: I don't know Paul, we're not in the land of Oz.

Paul: It's the starting point, that's what we were missing. We start with our only clue and follow it through.

Harry: I don't don't see where you're going with this.

Paul: The Doorman. He's our only link to whatever is beyond.

Harry: But he won't talk to you, you've tried that before.

Paul: Maybe I didn't ask him right.

Eric: He's not going to talk to you no matter how you ask him.

Paul: I'll force him to talk.

Harry: How?

Paul: We'll capture him.

(Everyone stares at Paul with stunned expressions.)

Harry: *(shaking his head)* I think you've finally flipped.

Paul: No wait, think it out. He's only one individual. All we have to do is wait for him behind the door and then pounce on him when he opens it.

Harry: What about the gun.

Paul: If we surprise him and grab him he won't be able to use it. And he can be surprised. Remember the look on his face when he found the Monk waiting for him.

Fred: I don't think that . . .

Paul: *(cutting Fred off)* You were right Fred. Once we've trapped the Doorman, we can force him to answer us.

Harry: Huh, I don't know.

Fred: What I meant was that . . . .

Paul: *(cutting Fred off again)* Harry it can work. I know it. He's our one real clue. He's our starting point.

Fred: Excuse me but aggression is an innate, instinctual aspect of the human experience. The Doorman is a catalyst to something outside of our experience.

Harry: He's right Paul, the Doorman can't answer your questions. He's just the guide to what's beyond the door.

            Your want to find meaning in this existence, but this world is only what our minds perceive it to be. What we see, feel and smell are all sensory elements that our brain interprets. But how do we know these interpretations are the same in my mind as they are in yours. Is it possible that this reality exists only because our minds make it so.

Boris: You cannot discount the pure reality of science with possible interpretations of sensory perception. The natural laws apply to all minds.

Harry: Science cannot explain sentient consciousness. If it were an evolutionary process, then why was it achieved by only one species in so brief a time of its existence. And if it was bequeathed by a Supreme Being, then why did He, She or They only give this gift to one species after an infinite amount of time.

Paul: We've got to give it a try. We've got to work together, one of us could be the next . . .

(Stage door left opens and the Doorman bursts in.)

Doorman: Hood . . . Harry Hood.

Paul: *(whirling around)* No! *(not a shout, more of a sad frustration)*

(A short pause, nobody moves.)

Doorman: Mr. Hood, it is time.

Paul: Don't go Harry.

Harry: I have to Paul, it's my time.

(Paul turns, hiding his emotions. Harry walks to the door, stops and turns to Paul.)

Harry: Paul, if I can, I'll try to reach you from wherever I am. Open your spiritual self and listen for me. I will try to make contact, I promise.

(Paul turns and rushes to Harry, embracing him in his arms.)

Doorman: *(calmly)* Mr. Hood, we must go.

Harry: Goodbye Paul.

(Harry turns and walks out the door with the Doorman.)

Fred: Illusions are often more preferable as they can mask the pain of our reality.

Boris: Science is the single light of knowledge, but when you meet an individual that is able to bring out the light within themselves, then they brighten the whole world with their illumination.

(Walking over to Paul and putting a hand on his shoulder.)

           A person cannot defend against suffering when that person freely loves.

(Elvis stands up from behind the bar, adjusts his clothes and walks to the front of the bar. Sally rises from behind the bar, adjusts her clothes and walks over to Elvis.)

Sally: *(nonchalantly)* So you're an Elvis Presley impersonator.

Elvis: Yup, I'm one of them, even legally changed my name to his.

Sally: Was there ever a real one, an original?

Elvis: Yes ma'am, there surely was. He came from
           Alpha Centauri, the first one. Double bourbon,
           straight, no ice. The rest of us just wish we
           came from Alpha Centauri. By the way, do
           you have any crossword puzzles?

Sally: That's a pretty stiff drink (passing him the glass).

Elvis: I'm a pretty stiff drinker (gulping it down).

Sally: I guess you're the proof that thousands of
           people have lived wonderful, fulfilling, exciting
           lives without ever once being themselves.

Elvis: What's so great about being yourself. Another
           double honey.

Sally: Is that why you drink?

Elvis: I came, I conquered, got bored, got lost,
           got drunk.

Sally: Some answer.

Elvis: Some question.

Sally: How about the truth?

Elvis: What is truth?

Sally: Perhaps truth is the basis of reality.

Elvis: I have but one reality, the bottle.

Sally: But why choose this reality?

Elvis: 'Cause I can't take the others.

Sally: Which are?

Elvis: Truth.

Sally: A paradox?

Elvis: No, not a paradox, just disappointment.

Sally: Not for everybody.

Elvis: That's why we're not all drunks.

Sally: Sounds reasonable.

Elvis: To a drunk, everything sounds reasonable.

Sally: Unless the bottle is empty.

Elvis: The bottle is rarely empty.

Sally: And when it is?

Elvis: Have you ever tried to take a drink from an empty bottle?

Sally: Not yet.

Elvis: Don't bother, you won't like the taste. Another bourbon please.

Sally: Haven't I served you enough already.

Elvis: You know, I've been served by many women, but I have to say that you are one magical hound dog.

Sally: I'm not sure if that's an insult or a compliment.

Fred: *(moving over to the bar to join them)* Insults can be compliments to the socially incompetent and compliments are a soothing lotion for a tattered ego. I believe the first truly civilized human being was the man who learned how throw insults instead of rocks.

Elvis: Basic human psychology, plus a bourbon straight.

Sally: *(while fixing a drink and says with a huff)*
           Human psychology. What does anyone really
           know about what's happening within the brain
           of another. Are we all motivated by sex or does
           our obsession with it create the need for it as
           a motivator.

Fred: Obsession can be the motivation for
           possession.

Elvis: Isn't that what life is? A journey from obsession
           to possession and back again. Do you have a
           menu?

Boris: Obsession can be a healthy attribute to
           accomplishment.

Sally: All my life I've been obsessed with sex and
           magic. There were a few times when I actually
           achieved multiple accomplishments, but even
           those faded with memory.

Boris: An accomplishment is something that has a
           lasting benefit. Your so-called accomplishments
           are nothing more than erotic confessions to
           temporary stimulus.

Sally: *(passing a menu)* When I go to confession
           I want the Priest to faint, the Rabbi to run
           screaming from my revelations, and the Imam
           to drop on his knees facing Mecca and praying
           to erase my testimony from his mind.

Boris: Now that would be an accomplishment.

Elvis: What about what we just accomplished behind
           the bar?

Sally: Sorry loverboy, but I think our accomplishment has already achieved all the magic it's going to generate.

Elvis: Are you dumping me already? I thought we had something special. I thought we had a relationship.

Sally: I don't have relationships with imitations. The batteries are too expensive.

Elvis: Aw honey, that's cruel, why can't you be easy on me. Why can't relationships just be beautiful, and simple. Oh, and can I have another bourbon?

Paul: *(to Boris)* We can catch him, I know we can.

Boris: You can't catch the Doorman!

Paul: You said it yourself, everything is based on a natural set of laws. Don't those laws apply to him as well?

Boris: I don't know, he's from outside the Pub.

Eric: If he's from outside of nature, then he must be un-natural.

Paul: That's right Eric, and we would need to work in an un-natural way to talk with him.

Sally: I've been un-natural for years and he's never spoken to me.

Paul: *(walking around, talking to all)* We can take him, I know we can. We can hold him until he tells us something, anything, even just a sense of what's beyond. Elvis can stand behind the door and hold it open.

Fred and I will grab him and drag him away
from the door. Then we can force him to talk. If
we have to, Boris can bash him with his SF
6900.

Boris: I'm not sure of this.

Paul: What's the worse that can happen.

Eric: He could call your name.

Fred: Well, he is going to call all of our names
eventually. Okay Paul, you've convinced me.
I'm willing to explore this option.

Elvis: What the hell *(drinks his shot)* I'm game.

Paul: Alright, we stand together. Let's get into
position. All we have to do is wait.

*(They get into position and wait, Elvis behind the door,
Fred and Paul beside the door.)*

Elvis: *(to Fred)* My mamma raised me to be a believer
in the Supreme Being. I ain't never questioned
or doubted what my mamma taught me.

Fred: No one can truly be forced to believe unless
they already have the propensity to fall into that
coercion. On the other hand, no one can be
forced to un-believe either.

Elvis: All the teachers who have faith in the Supreme
Being preach about love, charity and peace.
Those are good things; why do we need to
believe in anything else.

Fred: If everyone took these teachings to heart and
followed their ideals, then we probably
wouldn't be seeking answers, or even raising
the questions.

Elvis: When one is summoned by a higher power,
            then one must submit to the grace that is
            bestowed.

Fred: How does one give themself over to the
            ineffable?

Elvis: Happens every day. People willingly die for
            their beliefs.

Fred: But it is only belief, not one clearly proven
            piece of factual evidence.

Elvis: Just as the scientist believes in the probability
            of quantum theory, or the unified relativity of
            all things in the universe. For all we truly know,
            the earth is the centre of the universe and the
            Supreme Being has surrounded it with a canvas
            of cosmic beauty that orbits around us.

Fred: Touché.

Paul: Quiet, I think I hear something.

(Doorman bursts in through the door on stage right. All the others turn in disbelief.)

Doorman: Johnson . . . Eric Johnson.

Eric: Well it's about time! What took you so long?

(Eric rises begins to move to the stage left door.)

Doorman: This way Mr. Johnson, this way.

(Eric turns and taps his way to stage door right and follows the Doorman out the door.)

Boris: Well that was a waste of my time. I could have
            been working on my theory of Pub creation
            based on a singular event like an expanding
            balloon . . . a sort of Big Blow Up Pub theory.

Fred: Sir, I have empathy with your frustration. Personally I've spent years researching the feminine mystique.

Sally: Hey, Mr. Psycho – ANAL – ist.

Fred: That's analyst.

Sally: Whatever. All you had to do was ask me. End of research.

Paul: *(with desperation)* No wait, we can't give up now.

Boris: Paul, your trying to grasp onto something that comes from beyond our reality with hands that are confined to this reality.

Paul: No I mean it. If we watch both doors, there's no way he can escape us again. There's four of us *(looking at Sally)* five if you're in with us.

Sally: Not me, I like my job here just fine.

Paul: Alright, that makes two of us at each door. One grabs the door and one grabs the Doorman. The other two will then rush over to help. Boris and I will watch this door, Elvis and Fred will watch that one.

(They all take up positions.)

Fred: Tell me more about your mother.

Elvis: Not much to tell, she was a good mother, took care of us kids, always made sure we had a place to sleep and food to eat.

Fred: Did she ever give you a beating.

Elvis: Only when I deserved it.

Fred: When parents pass on their wisdom to their children, they also leave another inheritance, they also pass on their fears, their ignorance and their misfortune.

(Doorman bursts in through the door leading to the toilet.)

Doorman: Presley . . . Elvis Presley.

(All the others at the other doors turn in disbelief.)

Elvis: You want me to come with you into the bathroom?

(Doorman just stares at him.)

Sally: Here's your opportunity to find Alpha Centauri. Want a fried peanut butter and banana sandwich to take with you. *(hands him a brown paper bag)*

Elvis: Thank you, thank you very much. *(he accepts the bag from Sally and follows the Doorman into the bathroom)*

(The others mill around and commence to return to their seats. Paul, with a depressed sluggish movement returns back to the table and sits slouched.)

Sally: *(to Paul)* I'm pretty sure he's not the one you want.

Paul: How do you know?

Sally: I think the Doorman is just a release from our problems.

Paul: I don't understand.

Sally: I remember reading the story of an ancient
           mystic who taught that all life was suffering,
           and that to find peace was to learn how to
           overcome the suffering.

Paul: And then what? You try to overcome the
           torment of this existence and then follow the
           Doorman regardless of where he takes you.
           I still don't see any purpose to it all.

Boris: If you probe down to the atomic basics, then
           the properties of our bodies lose meaning.
           Things like colour, warmth, shape, firmness and
           even suffering are simply the illusions of atomic
           unity. What purpose could there be if we are
           nothing more than a random collection of
           gravitational forces.

           We are the evolution of everything past, and
           we are evolving into the future.

Fred: After all has been said, after all our actions are
           complete, nothing can withstand logic and
           reason.

Sally: Except that which is illogical and has no reason.

*(Sally comes from behind the bar to the centre of the
stage, facing the audience. The lights slowly dim.)*

Sally: I snap my finger and produce a flame. *(spotlight
           shines on her)*

           A simple trick, to amuse people, to get their
           attention.

           You look at me quizzically, wondering what I'm
           talking about.

           Don't shy away . . . . stay . . . . . stay and watch.

> This is good magic . . . . magic that will make
> you smile.

(Throughout Sally's words, the lights slowly fade except for a single spotlight on Paul as he walks towards front stage right. All the stage is now dark except for the spotlight on Paul as he stands alone, front stage right. From stage left, a Cloaked Figure comes in silently and stands front stage left. Another spotlight then shines on him as well.)

Cloaked
Figure: Mr. Satin, I hear you've been looking for me.

Paul: Who are you?

Cloaked
Figure: Well, I once told somebody "I am that I am."

Paul: Are you the Proprietor?

Cloaked
Figure: I've been called by many names. Godfrey,
Gail, Allan, and some I wouldn't care to
repeat in public. My favourite was "the Force."
However, there are some that don't call me
anything at all.

Paul: Why I am here?

Cloaked
Figure: You know, I get asked that a lot.

Paul: Why are any of us here?

Cloaked
Figure: *(sighs)* If I just simply gave you an answer, then
what would be the point of living. Also, would
you be able to even trust my answer.
Nevertheless, I have a better question;
Is your reality a creation of mine, or is my
reality is a creation of yours.

We each have to figure this out on a personal level.

Paul: Is that all you can tell me? That doesn't help. I need to know.

Cloaked
Figure: Paul, the hardest part is not searching for the answer. The hardest part is living the answer once you have found it.

(Lights fade out, curtain closes.)

CPSIA information can be obtained
at www.ICGtesting.com
Printed in the USA
BVHW071806040221
599249BV00006B/1189